CB007674

Richard Simonetti

WHO IS AFRAID OF DEATH ?

Translated by
Marilda Cortez Cesar Caselato

ISBN 85-86359-16-5
Cover Designer: José Policena de Campos Neto
Illustrations: Celso da Silva

Original Brazilian title:
" Quem Tem Medo da Morte?"

First edition in English – March 1999

Copyright 1999 by
Centro Espírita Amor e Caridade
Bauru São Paulo Brazil

Edition and Distribution

Rua Sete de Setembro, 8-56
CEP 17015-031
Bauru São Paulo Brazil
Tel/fax +55-14-2270618
www.ceac.org.br
ceac@ceac.org.br

CATALOGED IN THE RECORDS
OF
THE NATIONAL BOOK DEPARTMENT

S598w
Simonetti, Richard, 1935-
  Who is afraid of death? / Richard
Simonetti. 1. ed. - Bauru, SP : CEAC
Ed, 1999.
  144p. : il. ; cm

  ISBN 85-86359-16-5.

  1. Espiritismo. 2. Medo da Morte. I.
Título.

CDD-133.9

"Let us look at the dead ones as if they were just absent. By thus thinking, we will not be mistaken."

(Seneca)

"Death is nothing more than the return to the real life."

(Scipio)

"Nothing vanishes and nothing dies, except the coating, the shape, the carnal envelope, in which the confined Spirit struggles, fights, suffers, improves. The shape dies - the carcass - but the soul shines again - the gnome of light; and what is this existence of the body - a single blow - in face of the existence of the soul - the eternity? We are the dead ones; dead in life, in order to live again in death."

(Alberto Veiga)

TABLE OF CONTENT

Preface 13
Beam of Light 15
The Spiritual Body 19
Spiritual Help 24
Disconnection 27
Balance 30
Difficulties in the Return Journey 34
The Rally from Death 37
Unfailing Resource 40
Delays in the Disconnecting Process 43
Tragedy 46
Compromising Escape 49
Death of Children 53
Why Do Flowers Die? 57
Abortion 60
Awareness of Wrongdoing 64
A Disgusting Solution 67
Old Trauma 71
Is It Time? 75
Dangerous Game 78
Funerals 81
Ideal Funeral 85

For His Sake 88
The Garment in the Closet 91
Warnings from Beyond 94
Strange Cult 98
Flowers for the Dead 101
Cremation 104
Transplants 108
Blessed Charity 112
Curious Obsession 116
The Most Important 119
Roots of Stability 123
Returned Jewels 126
Passport 130

ACKNOWLEDGMENTS

Thanks to the people who made
possible the English Edition
of this book.

In Brazil
Ângela Maria Ferreira de Freitas
Marcelo and Cláudia Palhares
Maria Aparecida Tuon

In the USA
Daniel Benjamin
George and Akemi Adams
Jussara Korngold

Special Thanks
to Sidney Francez Fernandes
for the general coordination
of this project.

PREFACE

"To free yourself of the fear of death one must be able to face it under its true aspect. In other words, to have penetrated in thought in the spiritual world, making of it as precise an idea as possible."
(Allan Kardec)

A few years ago I lectured about the circumstances related to the return to the Spiritual World during a seminar about death held in Brazil, in the city of Bauru.

I was surprised at the interest of the audience. Many questions were raised.

There are many doubts and much fear, even from religious people, since the traditional knowledge about death is speculative, based on assumptions from medieval theologians.

The same happened in other cities where the same lecture was presented. Many people with many questions related to suicide, fatal accidents, disconnection, death of children, organ donation, cremation, cemeteries, euthanasia, abortion, murders, imprudence, addictions, premonition...

There were so many questions that it was not possible to answer all of them. Then, I had the idea of writing a book where the most frequent questions about death would be answered. It had to be a first reader on the subject, something that would be interesting to everyone, regardless of religious belief, since no one is exempt from a direct or indirect contact with it, in the form of one's own death or the death of a beloved family member.

In an attempt to make it a first reader, I have avoided highly technical concepts, as well as an erudite approach.

The essence, however, is faithful to the principles of the Spiritist Doctrine, as codified by Allan Kardec, the blessed source where we seek guidance to face life's difficulties and death's enigmas.

Finally, I will be very pleased if this English edition helps someone else "kill" death, by overcoming fears and doubts and by understanding that death is only the passport needed for our return to the common nation, the Spiritual Realms.

BEAM OF LIGHT

Late at night, a man was walking along a deserted road. The night was dark, no moonlight, dimmed stars. He was worried. There had been many thefts in that area... He noticed someone following him.

- "Hello! Who is it?" - he asked, frightened.

He got no answer. He hurried on, but his follower imitated him. He ran... So did the stranger. In panic, as he ran as fast as his legs would allow him to, his heart beating wildly, his lungs burning, he passed by a beam of light. He looked back and, as if by magic, the fear vanished. His chaser was but an old donkey which was used to following wanderers.

This story is similar to what happens in relation to death. Immortality is something intuitive to the human being. Nevertheless, many people are afraid of it because they are totally unaware of the process they will have to go through and what will be awaiting for them in the spiritual world.

The religions, which should prepare the believers for life beyond the grave, making them conscious of the soul's survival, unveiling the curtains that separate the two worlds, do very little in this regard. They limit themselves to the fields of fantasy.

The Spiritist Doctrine is the "beam of light" that sheds its light on the mysterious paths of return, chasing away irrational fears and disturbing embarrassments. Through the lenses of the Spiritism we can look at death peacefully, as we prepare ourselves to face it. This is extremely important, truly fundamental, since death is the only certainty of the human existence: **we all shall die one day**!

Our planet Earth is a workshop for those who are engaged in enlightening activities, promoting their own renewal; a hospital for those who need to make up for disagreements stemmed from old addictions; a painful prison for those paying for crimes committed in a previous existence; a school for those who have already understood that life is not merely a biological accident nor the human existence a simple recreational journey. Earth is not our home. Our home is the spirit world, where we can live wholeheartedly, without the limitations imposed by the flesh.

Thus, it is easy to understand that we have to prepare ourselves by overcoming fears and doubts, restlessness and mistakes, so that when our time comes we may be ready for a balanced and peaceful return.

The first step towards such achievement is to dissociate that dismal, morbid, fearful, supernatural aspect from death... There is an age-old conditioning towards that. There are people who simply refuse to conceive the idea of a family member's death or even their own. They relegate the subject to a very distant future. Therefore, when the time for separation comes, they are totally unprepared.

"Where, O death, is your sting?" - asks Paul, the apostle, (I Corinthians 15:55), demonstrating to us that faith overcomes all fears and anguishes caused by the great transition. Spiritism likewise offers us the necessary resources to face death with similar strength, inspired by faith. Faith which is not based on a flight of emotions, but a logical reasoned conscious faith. It is the steadfast faith of those who are aware of, and know what is awaiting them, and work hard in order to have the best possible return.

THE SPIRITUAL BODY

It is amazing how resistant people are to the expression "to disincarnate". This resistance seems to be acceptable for a materialistic person. After all, for him everything ends at the grave... This should not be the same for those who believe in eternal life, regardless of religion. If we accept that the individuality outlives the death of the physical body, the expression will then impose itself as being the description of the process that frees the Spirit of the flesh.

For a better understanding of this subject, it is imperative to consider the existence of the spiritual body or perispirit, as explained by Allan Kardec in "The Spirits' Book", questions 150 and 150-a:

"Does the soul preserve its individuality after death?"

"Yes, it never loses its identity. What would the soul be without an identity?"

"How does the soul assert its individuality, since it no longer has a material body?"

"It still has a semi-material body peculiar to itself, which it draws from the atmosphere of its planet and which represents the appearance of its last incarnation - its perispirit."

Questions 135 and 135-a are also very enlightening:

"Is there anything in human beings besides a soul and a body?"

"Yes, there is the link by which the soul and the body are connected."

"Can you describe this link?"

"It is semi-material. In other words, it is by nature midway between soul and body. Without it, soul and body could not communicate with each other. This is, in fact, the purpose of the link: it enables the spirit to act on matter and matter to act on the spirit."

Allan Kardec remarks:

"A human being is formed of three essential elements:

1. The body, which humans have in common with animals. As such, the body is animated by the same vital principle that exists in animals;

2. The soul, or incarnate spirit, of which the body is the habitation and through which it acts;

3. The semi-material form called the perispirit; it constitutes the spirit's innermost envelope and unites the spirit with the body.

It might help to think of this triad-like arrangement in terms of the structure of a peach or an apricot. At the core of these fruits there is a nucleus, i.e., an inner germ, which we can think of as the spirit. The nucleus is surrounded by a stone or perisperm, which in us is analogous to the perispirit. The Stone, in turn, is surrounded by the edible flesh of the fruit, which is comparable to our body."

Since ancient times, researchers have admitted the existence of an extra-corporeal body, a vehicle for the manifestation of the Spirit in the level it acts. (In the physical world to link it to the flesh, and in the spiritual world to adapt it to the characteristics and beings of the realms where it resides.)

Paul, the apostle, refers to the perispirit as he reports in the II Epistle to the Corinthians (12:2 to 4). "I know a man in Christ, who fourteen years ago was caught up to the third heaven. Whether it was in the body or out of the body, I do not know - God knows. And I know that this man - whether in the body or apart from the body I do not know, but God knows - was caught up to Paradise. He heard inexpressible things, things that man is not permitted to tell."

While his physical machine was put to sleep in order to get the necessary rest, Paul, in his spiritual body, traveled to the Upper Worlds, conducted by friendly benefactors, in order to receive important teachings. Trying to define the nature of his experience, he commented in the Epistle to the Corinthians (15:40): "There are heavenly bodies and earthly bodies."

Such displacements are not a privilege of saints. All human beings experience them daily while they are asleep, but we are only able to retain fragmented and fleeting memories in the form of dreams. We must consider, though, that the nature of those excursions is determined by the kind of activities that we perform while we are awake. That is why the ordinary man, so entangled with immediate pleasures, weaknesses and ambitions, who is completely indifferent to spiritual self-improvement and disciplined emotions, is not able to go through such sublime experiences as the one reported by Paul.

We all "die", everyday, during our sleep. However, in order to wander safely and consciously in the spirit realms, taking full advantage of these moments for learning, working and progressing, it is necessary to cultivate Spiritual values during the waking hours. Otherwise we will feel like fish out of water in the spiritual world.

SPIRITUAL HELP

The word "disconnection" is a good definition for the disincarnating process. To set itself free, the Spirit must be disconnected from the physical body, since we remain linked to it by the fluid bonds that sustain our union with matter.

Due to the need for specialized service, similar to what happens in any human activity, there are spiritual technicians who approach the disincarnating person, and by magnetic means bring about the disengagement. Only highly evolved beings do not require this type of assistance. This means that we can always count on specialized help during our transition, in addition to the comforting presence of relatives and friends who have preceded us.

Obviously, the greater or lesser spiritual help provided is determined by the merits of the disincarnating person. If the person is virtuous and dignified he/she will deserve special attention and once the disincarnating process is over he will be conducted to assistance institutions that will favor his/her readaptation to the Spiritual Life. On the other hand, those people entangled with addictions and crimes, who lacked discipline and discernment, will be disconnected at the proper time, but will be left to their fate, remaining indefinitely in the lower realms, a dark belt that surrounds the Earth, formed by the mental vibrations of multitudes of incarnate and disincarnate Spirits that are still dominated by primitive impulses of bestiality.

The religious tradition established the extreme unction, when, through rites and prayers, an officiator absolves the sins, preferably confessed by the moribund, assuring him a nice arrival in the spirit world.

Nevertheless, the reality depicted by the Spiritist Doctrine is totally different. Verbal and ritualistic formulas have no effect in the domains of Death. The same is true with the formal repentance which reflects more the fear of afterlife punishments than the consciousness of the spiritual impoverishment.

The prodigal son, as told by Jesus in His memorable parable, stayed away from the comfort of his home, facing a distressing situation, until he realized how miserable his life was, more depriving than the life of the most humble of his father's servants. He decided then to begin the long journey back home. To his surprise, the father received him with immense joy.

We are all sons of God, created to His image and likeness, provided with His creative potentialities and intrinsically destined to Good. Nevertheless, we become candidates for long periods of suffering in the inferior realms, every time we engage ourselves in wrongdoing, but one day, like the prodigal son, we sincerely repent and return to the paths of the Lord, starting the arduous journey of renovation.

DISCONNECTION

Disincarnation, in other words, the process through which the Spirit, enveloped by a perispirit, leaves the body, is still inaccessible to the present Earth Science, since it happens in the spiritual dimension where no scientific device, no matter how sophisticated it may be, has been able to penetrate.

Therefore we remain limited to the information received from the Spirits who in turn are limited by the difficulties imposed by our human barriers (something like explaining the functioning of the endocrine system to a child), and also by the lack of similarity (elements for comparison between the biological and spiritual phenomena).

Leaving the technical details aside, we can say that the disincarnating process starts in the extremities of the body and reaches completion as the fluid bonds that link the Spirit to the body are undone.

It is known that the dying person has cold hands and feet, a circulatory phenomenon, explained by the weakening of the heart that can no longer pump the blood adequately. But that is also a disconnecting phenomenon. As it progresses, the corresponding areas no longer receive the vital fluid that emanates from the Spirit and sustains the physical organization.

During this process, the disconnection of the fluid bond that ties the Spirit to the body at heart level causes the latter to lose the spiritual support and to stop beating. The blood circulation ceases and death occurs in no time.

Today, medical science has got a large number of devices to reanimate a patient when his heart collapses. Cardiac massage, electrical shock, and intracardiac adrenaline shots have saved thousands of lives when applied at once, before the brain cells begin to degenerate by lack of oxygen.

Those treatments are efficient when related to a mere functional problem, such as a heart attack, lack of blood circulation in certain areas of the heart, caused by thrombosis or artery clogging. The heart attack may lead to disincarnation, but this does not necessarily mean that the time for the patient to die has come. There are frequent cases where patients are revived by means of medical assistance.

However when the heart attack is caused by the disconnection of the fluid bond, not even the most skilled doctor, using the most modern medical devices, will be able to reanimate the patient. This is an irreversible process.

BALANCE

The imminence of death starts up a curious reminiscence process. The dying person relives, during a very brief lapse of time, the emotions of a lifetime, which are projected in his mind like the images of an extraordinary movie, running at a vertiginous speed.

It is a kind of life balance, a survey of credits and debts in the divine accounting which will define the ranking of the Spirit as he returns to the spiritual world, based on good and bad deeds. However, the values to be counted in his favor are those that "moths cannot destroy and thieves cannot steal", as instructed by Jesus, and which were acquired by his Good Deeds.

This is an automatic psychological mechanism that can be triggered in the inner levels of consciousness without the occurrence of death. There are frequent cases in which the dying person comes back to life, spontaneously, or by means of various resources.

Many doctors have been researching the subject, especially in the United States where Dr. Raymond Moody Jr. is an outstanding name. In his book "Life After Life", he describes the experiences of several people who were reported to be clinically dead.

It is important to emphasize that these accounts confirm the information given by the Spiritist Doctrine. The people interviewed talk about the "balance" of their existence. They also mention topics well known to the Spiritists: the spiritual body or perispirit, the difficulty to recognize their own "death" situation, the contact with the spiritual guides and relatives, the ability of "feeling" what people are thinking, the ability to float with incredible sense of weightlessness, the vision of their own dead body and the extremely uncomfortable impressions felt by those who tried to commit suicide.

The studies revealed that such phenomena frequently occur to different patients, who generally keep silent, for fear of being considered mentally ill.

In the book "The Gospel According to Spiritism", Allan Kardec states that the universality of the Spiritist principles (similarity in the Spirits' communications, obtained from numerous mediums in several countries) testifies to its authenticity, since such great coincidence would have been impossible.

Likewise, the authenticity of Dr. Moody's research is statistically corroborated by the reports of hundreds of patients who have come back from Beyond and who mention the same elements we have just mentioned, in spite of having different religious backgrounds, being from different cultural and social levels, and living in different areas.

The experience of reviewing his own existence in such dramatic circumstances may represent a unique admonition to the revived person, making him aware of the need to "invest" in his spiritual renovation, so that he will not be considered "bankrupt" in the Spiritual World when his time really comes.

DIFFICULTIES IN THE RETURN JOURNEY

The progressive debility of the patient drives him into unconsciousness, which has the effect of a general anesthetic on the Spirit which, with very few exceptions, sleeps to die, remaining unaware of the great transition.

Levelheaded people with a surplus of good deeds overcome the "anesthetic of death" and can perfectly watch the work being performed by the spiritual technicians. This can cause some constraint, something like a patient watching himself undergoing a delicate surgery but, on the other hand, this will facilitate their integration to the new spiritual life. Once the disconnecting process is over, they will be totally conscious. The same does not happen to the ordinary man, who sleeps to die and awakes in a state of dizziness, somewhat agitated by the impressions of the material life, especially by those related to the circumstances of his death.

Spiritists who are familiar with the manifestations of suffering spirits during mediumistic sessions know this problem well. The communicating spirits are generally not aware of their new situation and complain about the indifference of relatives that do not pay much attention to them. They feel disturbed and afflicted. They were totally unprepared for the return journey and cannot free themselves of the experiences of the material life, feeling like fishes out of water, or to be more precise like mentally sick people who live in a world of fantasy, inside themselves.

This troubled state of mind will only be dissipated after some time. The help from spiritual guides and prayers of relatives and friends can accelerate the understanding, but, essentially, this will depend on the level of attachment to human fantasies and the capacity to assimilate the new reality.

The lack of preparation to face death is a natural thing for thousands of people who return daily to the spiritual world, not having the least idea of what is waiting for them, after decades of complete indifference to noble values. They have probably never stopped to consider the meaning of the Earth journey, where they come from, why they are here, or what their destiny is. Lacking the compass of faith and the luggage of good deeds, they remain astonished and confused.

To this regard, we have to admit that Spiritism is a blessed training course about the realities of life after death. The Spiritist, supported by the extensive and precise instructions received, will be able to land more safely on the invisible continent. He will not have major problems recognizing the new situation, even though that information will not grant him the right to go into more fortunate communities. This will depend on what he did and not on what he knows.

The "account balance of death" will define whether we have accumulated enough virtues to afford the tickets to higher spheres, and the Spiritist will be requested to pay interest for the knowledge acquired since, according to the Law, "more will be asked from those who received more".

THE RALLY FROM DEATH

The strongest feeling when we face the death of a dear one is the feeling of loss.

"My husband cannot die! He is my mainstay! He is my safety"

"My dear wife! Do not leave me alone! I cannot live without you!

"My son, my son! Do not go! You are so young! What will become of me not having you by my side when I grow old?"

It is amazing how people do not worry about the dying person himself. Even those who accept life after death pray unceasingly, refusing to admit the separation. This kind of behavior goes beyond affection and leads us into the old human selfishness, somewhat like a prisoner that refuses to accept the idea that his cell mate is going to be set free.

The exaggeration of grief expressed by despair and non-acceptance creates fluid bonds that weave a retention web where the physical life is artificially sustained. Such vibrations will not prevent death, they will only put it off, making the disincarnating person go through a lot more suffering.

It is normal for us, in face of a serious problem that affects a beloved person, to experience feelings of apprehension and anguish. Nevertheless, it is mandatory for us not to let ourselves be led into hatred and despair, which always increase the human problems, especially those related to death.

When the family members refuse to accept the separation, thus creating the undesirable vibration web, the Spiritual Benefactors, through magnetic resources, artificially recover the dying patient. Then, an unexpected recovery occurs and he regains consciousness and is able to mutter a few words.

That treatment is usually effected during the late hours, when the family members, exhausted but relieved, decide to take a rest.

"Thank God! The Lord has listened to our prayers!", they proclaim.

Taking advantage of the truce, the spiritual benefactors accelerate the disincarnating process and the disconnection begins. Death comes then to escort more passengers into the spiritual world.

Few people realize the need to help the disincarnating person during the traumatic transition. That is why this procedure is frequently used by the spiritual Guides, sending away those who not only do not help, but make things even worse. There is even a popular saying about the subject:

"It was the rally from death!" they say. "He got better to die."

UNFAILING RESOURCE

Death, except on rare occasions, is a traumatic process. After all, the Spirit has to leave behind a vehicle of flesh to which it is so intimately connected, it seems an inseparable part of its individuality (or the individuality itself to materialists).

On the other hand, only very few are ready for this compulsory journey, when we leave the small island of physical perceptions on a course towards the glorious continent of spiritual truths. Impregnated by material interests and concerns, the travelers have to face understandable hindrances.

Under such circumstances, both the patient, who gradually becomes weaker, and the family members, who go through a painful mourning, can make use of an unfailing resource, the prayer.

Because of its eminently spiritual characteristics, representing an effort to overcome the Earthly conditionings for a communion with Heaven, the prayer favors a nice "trip" for those who are departing the physical world. For those who stay, it brings a soothing relief that reduces the personal feeling of loss and fills the gap left in the heart with the comforting presence of God, blessed source of confidence, balance and serenity in every situation.

However, its effectiveness is subordinated to one essential condition: the feeling we add to it. If we simply repeat words in oral formulas, we fall into an innocuous process. Only the heart is able to communicate with God, and it can do it without verbalization.

Even the sublime prayer taught by Jesus, "The Lord's Prayer" is not a magic tool whose efficiency is subject to repetition. It is an itinerary to be followed as we pray. It begins by telling us to be very confident because God is our father, and it ends by inciting us to defeat the evil inside us by systematically combating the temptations.

We should give special emphasis to that incisive sentence "Thy will be done, in Earth as in Heaven", through which Jesus stresses that it is up to God to define what is better for us. Under any circumstance, especially in that of the great transition, if we nurture feelings of despair and nonacceptance, the prayer will not do any good and the uneasiness will remain.

When the disincarnating person and his family manage to control the emotions, cultivating, through prayer, feelings of confidence and humbleness, the Spiritual Benefactors are able to easily further the disconnection, with no major traumas for the dying one and with no despair for those who stay.

DELAYS IN THE DISCONNECTING PROCESS

Physical death and disincarnation do not occur simultaneously. The person dies when the heart stops beating. The Spirit disincarnates when the disconnecting process is completed, which requires a few hours or a few days.

Basically the Spirit remains bonded to the body while the impressions from his physical existence are very strong. Materialistic people, who take up the human journey as an end in itself, who do not establish higher goals and cultivate addictions and passions, remain attached longer, until the impregnated gross fluid, with which they are permeated, is reduced to levels compatible with the disconnecting process.

It is obvious that the spiritual benefactors can release the Spirit immediately after the physical death. Nevertheless, this is not advisable because the dying person would have even greater difficulties in adjusting to the spiritual reality. What apparently seems to be a kind of punishment for the individual who has not lived according to moral and virtuous principles is a simple act of mercy. Despite the constraint and unpleasant sensations he might feel at the sight of his disintegrating dead body, such circumstances are less traumatic than the immediate disconnection.

There are misconceptions about death which are totally different from reality. When someone dies from a sudden heart attack, people usually say:

"What a wonderful death! He did not suffer!

However, this is not a desirable death. When someone dies in full vitality, except if highly spiritualized, he will face disconnection and adaptation problems, because the impressions and interests associated to his material existence will be very strong in him.

When death is a consequence of cancer after a long period of suffering, caused by sharp pains through which the patient slowly decays, fading away while alive, people say:

"What a terrible death! So much suffering!"

Paradoxically, this is a good death. A prolonged disease is like a beauty treatment to the Spirit. The physical pains serve as an invaluable therapeutic resource, helping the person to get over worldly illusions, in addition to purging, as a drain valve, the moral impurities. Notice that as the patient gradually gets worse, he becomes more receptive to religious appeals, to the benefits of prayers, to meditations on the human fate. That is why, when death comes, he is more prepared and even awaits for it with no bonds nor fears.

Something similar occurs to people who die very old, after fulfilling the time granted by the Divine Law, and leading a disciplined and virtuous life. For them, the physical life is extinguished placidly, like a candle that flickers and is extinguished, after being totally used, granting them a peaceful return journey, without major difficulties.

TRAGEDY

Thousands of people return to the Spiritual World everyday, entangled in tragic circumstances: fire, landslide, earthquake, drowning, car and airplane accidents....

"Why?"- the anguished family members ask.

The Spiritist Doctrine demonstrates that such occurrences are associated with evolutionary experiences. Not rarely they are the payment of karmic debts stemming from violent acts in the past.

We are all shaken when such tragedies involve our beloved ones. Many people, disoriented, plunge into a crisis of despair and revolt, an understandable reaction in face of the unexpected impact. Only the unceasing flowing of time, day after day, will ease the pain and make people return to their normal activities. Life goes on...

However, the disincarnated person cannot wait. He is the focus of the tragedy and remains bewildered and puzzled. Even though assisted by the spiritual guides, he faces enormous problems of adaptation and suffers, reflecting the feelings of his family members. If they insist in cultivating unhappy memories, keeping in their minds the painful details of the tragedy, this will undoubtedly force the Spirit to persistently revive the agony of his death. Let's imagine someone who died in a fire and is forced to unceasingly see himself in a hell of flames generated by the tormented thoughts of those who are reluctant to his death...

In communications from such Spirits there is a constant plea for their family members to return to their normal activities and to develop new habits, particularly those related to good deeds - a divine balm that helps to soothe the pain of separation.

In the book "Life Beyond Death", written through the medium Francisco Cândido Xavier, the spirit of the young William Jose Guagliardi, who died with other fifty-eight people when their school bus plunged into a river, in São José do Rio Preto, Brazil, sends his mother the following message, trying to comfort her:

"I am here, begging you please to help me with your patience. I've been suffering more because of your tears than with the liberation of my body... Mother, your pain keeps me bonded to the reminiscence of my drowning and when you start wondering how the accident could have occurred, in your silent despair, I feel the suffocation again."

Of course we will not be able to keep an unemotional peacefulness, considering it natural to see a beloved one die so tragically. However ample our understanding may be, we will certainly suffer a lot. Maybe there is no worse anguish than this. It is mandatory, however, that we keep a serene attitude, cultivating our trust in God, not only for our own benefit, but above all, for the benefit of the one who has left us. More than ever he needs our help.

COMPROMISING ESCAPE

Undoubtedly, of all the circumstances regarding death, the most tragic one is the suicide, which has devastating consequences to the disincarnating person. Far from being considered as a trial, in compliance with divine wishes, self destruction is a disastrous escape, a false door through which the individual, wishing to free himself of all his maladies, falls into a much worse situation.

"The greatest of all sufferings on Earth does not compare to ours."- invariably say the spirits of suicides, when communicating in mediumistic sessions.

They get trapped in unimaginable torments immediately after their deplorable act. Violently projected into the Spiritual World while still in full physical vitality, they experience unceasingly, during a long period of time, the pains and emotions of the last minutes. They remain trapped in dark regions where, according to the Gospel, "there will be weeping and gnashing of teeth..."

One of the biggest problems faced by a person who commits suicide is the violation caused to his perispirit. Those people, who die violently, against their will, keep in their perispirits the marks and impressions related to the type of death they went through. Those are, however, temporary and tend to disappear as soon as they are completely reintegrated in the Spiritual Life.

The same does not happen to the person who commits suicide, for he will show the wounds resulting from the aggression imposed upon his physical body. If he shot himself in the head, there will be a severe lesion in the corresponding area. If caustic soda was used, he will experience a vast ulceration of the digestive system. If he threw himself under a train, he will show generalized traumas.

Such effects that by and large contribute to the great suffering of self-killers, generally require reincarnation in a new physical structure for a complete recovery - a new incarnation which will fatally reflect those effects. The shot in the head will give rise to reasoning difficulties. The caustic soda will cause severe malfunctions of the digestive system. The violent impact under the wheels of the train will show through neurological problems.

As in all cases of violent death, the person who commits suicide will experience inevitable worsening of his sufferings if the family members remain desperate and in an unaccepting attitude, and many times this is even aggravated by their feeling of guilt.

"Oh! If only we had behaved differently! If we had been more attentive! If we had tried to understand him!"

It is useless to conjecture about the *fait accompli*. In the presence of a wounded person after a brutal and unexpected tragedy, it would be counterproductive to keep wondering what might not have happened had we acted differently. It has already happened and cannot be changed! We must remain calm and look after the patient.

The same occurs with the person who commits suicide. His spirit demands urgent help. It is mandatory for us to react against despair and to cultivate prayer. This act of devotion is a comforting balm, a new solace to his sufferings in the Spiritual World, the great healing capable of lifting him up.

And if it seems disorienting to ponder about the endless and painful experiences of the companion who decided to voluntarily leave, let us consider that his suffering will not be in vain. It is a hard lesson that will make him grow, make it possible for him to have respect for Life, and will make him seek God.

DEATH OF CHILDREN

When death occurs during childhood, even under tragic circumstances, it is much more peaceful because during this phase of life the Spirit remains in a kind of slumbering state, gradually waking up to his Earth existence. Only during adolescence he will be in full control of his capabilities.

Indifferent to the human events, he is not yet entangled in addictions and passions that so badly compromise the physical experience and make it more difficult to have a balanced return to the Spiritual Life.

The major problem is the retention web that is strongly woven, because the death of a child always causes great commotion even from those not directly involved. The little being is a symbol of purity and innocence, a joy in the present and a promise for the future, and so he encompasses the hopes of the adults who refuse to face the perspective of separation.

In order to help the disincarnating child it is necessary to behave somewhat like the character Amaro in the book "Between Heaven and Earth", dictated by the Spirit André Luiz through Francisco Cândido Xavier. At the prospect of his one-year-old child's death, late at night while the other family members are sleeping, he watches over the child and meditates. The author describes it as follows:

"Dawn was starting to reflect light into the firmament in the form of wide reddish stripes when the railroad worker stopped meditating and came closer to the agonizing little boy.

In a touching act of faith he picked up the old wooden crucifix from the wall and placed it by the child's bedside. Then he sat on the bed and tenderly took the son in his arms. Spiritually supported by Odila* , who was embracing him, he rested his eyes over the image of the Crucified Christ and prayed out loud:

"-Divine Jesus, have mercy on our weaknesses! My spirit is fragile to deal with death! Give us strength and understanding... Our children belong to you, but how painful it is when the time comes to give them back to you upon your will calling for their return!

The mourning hinders his voice, but the grieving father, showing his urgent necessity for prayer, goes on:

"-If it is your will that our little son departs, my Lord, take him in your arms of Love and Light! Grant us, however, the necessary courage to bravely bear our Cross made of pain and suffering from his absence! ... Give us resignation, faith, and hope! ... Help us to understand your purposes and may thy will be done today and forever! ...."

---

* Amaro is married a second time. Odila was his first wife, who has already died.

"A beam of sapphire-like light started to flow out of Amaro's chest and enveloped the child, who, little by little, fell asleep."

"Julio left his flesh body, and found comfort in Odila's arms, as an orphan seeking a nest of tenderness and affection."

The faithful attitude of Amaro, his profound trust in Jesus, helped him keep his self-control and favored the return of Julio, his beloved son, to the Spiritual World, **according to what was established**.

WHY DO FLOWERS DIE?

There is no room for chance in the human existence. God is not a gambler with dice, randomly distributing joy and sorrow, happiness and sadness, health and illness, life and death. There are laws enforced by God that rule the evolution of His creatures, providing them experiences compatible with their needs.

One of them is Reincarnation, determining that we shall live multiple lives in the flesh, as students periodically admitted to a boarding school for some specific learning.

Knowledge about reincarnation helps us to uncover the intricate problems of Destiny. God knows what he is doing when a little flower from the garden of life has to return to the Spiritual World.

Some people who commit suicide sometimes reincarnate for a brief journey. Their feeling of frustration after many years of hard preparation to return to flesh will help them to value the human existence and overcome the tendency of escaping from their problems through self-destruction. At the same time, the contact with the material world will be beneficial to the treatment of perispiritual maladjustment caused by the insane act. Children with severe congenital problems that lead to death perfectly fit this condition.

If necessary, after a period of time, they will reincarnate again in the same family in better health conditions and with greater disposition to face the trials on Earth. Many times the child born after the death of a sibling will show similar pattern of behavior with identical reactions and tendencies.

"He is just like his deceased brother!"-family members comment.

No, he is not just like! He is the very brother returning for a new learning journey...

There are also evolved Spirits who reincarnate with the purpose of awakening spiritual impulses in old friends - parents, brothers and sisters, helping them to overcome the attachment to the material life.

Due to their evolved conditions, they are generally adorable children - extremely nice, clever and loving. Parents dedicate to them their total affection and claim that the children are the main reason for their existence. When the children disincarnate, parents feel puzzled and aggrieved.

Nevertheless, as they emerge from the lassitude and despair, they start to experience the blessed detachment from human futility and feel the awakening of an unsuspected religious vocation, stimulated by their own children who, invisible to their eyes, can whisper deep into their hearts, tuned to their feelings of longing.

Those parents who cry over the coffin of a beloved child will eventually understand that the temporary separation is part of a spiritual evolution plan, which will give rise to a closer union, to a greater and long-lasting happiness after the glorious reencounter, **which will inexorably come**.

ABORTION

Right after the egg is fertilized by the spermatozoid, the reincarnating Spirit is connected to the embryo, forming the new being who will be in the mother's womb for the next nine months, protected in its fragile state until it is able to face the outside world. Therefore, abortion is considered a kind of disincarnation.

When there is a miscarriage - because the mother's body cannot sustain the child's development

- it is considered a trial due to breaches of the Divine Laws, both for parents, who see their parenthood expectations frustrated (for the woman there are the added constraints of physical pains and after-effects of an interrupted pregnancy), and also for the reincarnating spirit whose intent to return to a flesh body is cut short.

The criminal abortion, however, represents a hideous crime, which is not always punished by the human justice (in some countries the law grants women the right to expel the offspring from her belly, murdering it). But it is inexorably subject to the penalties of the Divine Justice, which will fall upon not only the pregnant woman but also on those directly or indirectly involved (family members who suggest the abortion and professionals who perform it).

The woman who kills the defenseless child while it is still in her womb, claiming to be the owner of her own body, applies a materialistic paradox. Our body is a loan from God for the human journey. We have more obligations than rights related to its use. The first one is to preserve it by using it with discipline, being aware of its needs. The second is to respect the life created inside of it, in conformity with the divine will, since the Creator is responsible for deciding upon the destiny of His creation.

The Spiritist literature gives us many examples of the dreadful consequences of a criminal abortion, which can severely harm the perispirit of the pregnant woman. This will, in turn, be manifested in her physical body during the current lifetime or in future ones in the form of cancer, infertility, recurring infections, and frigidity.

Health problems like these are very common nowadays, showing how greatly disseminated this criminal practice is. Many women even use abortive chemicals regularly every time the menstruation period is late, without checking whether they are pregnant or not. They sow afflictions that they will undoubtedly reap later...

In a miscarriage, the Spirit returns to the Spiritual World without major problems. The fluidic bonds that link him to the body are very subtle not only because it is the very beginning of a reincarnation process but also because in face of the problem that leads to the disincarnation, he is somewhat prepared like a terminal patient.

Once the disincarnation is complete, the Spirit is able to resume his former personality, returning to what he was with the gains of the brief experience. If he is not mentally mature for this, he will remain as a newborn in the Spiritual World, waiting for the lapse of time to enable him to recover consciousness, developing as a child, or getting ready for a new reincarnation.

In the criminal abortion the picture is more complex. The Spirit suffers the trauma caused by a violent death, although minimized by the fact that he is not compromised by the delusions of the world yet. But because this is an unplanned event, resulting from parents' lack of responsibility, his frustration will be greater.

The re-adaptation will be similar to that of the Spirit victim of a miscarriage. It should be taken into account, however, that if it is still morally immature, its forced expulsion might cause a bitter rage against its parents turning it into a restless chaser of those who refused to grant it the opportunity of a new life.

Many problems that torment the woman, after a criminal abortion, which last endlessly despite medical treatment, originate from this influence.

AWARENESS OF WRONGDOING

If, on the one hand, the light shed by the teachings of the Spiritist Doctrine is capable of preventing many women from inducing an abortion, the "intra-womb murder", on the other hand it may also be a source of torture for those who have performed one. Fear, regret, anguish, depression are some of the reactions. This is a natural reaction whenever we are informed of what is awaiting for us as a consequence of misbehavior.

However, those who consider the Spiritist Doctrine the revival of thrashing, eschatological and anathematizing doctrines are totally mistaken.

Spiritism is based on logic and reasoning, and praises the freedom of consciousness. Spiritism never condemns - it enlightens; it does not threaten - it makes you aware. More than revealing what is bad in man, it aims at helping him find the Good within.

We are all immature Spirits still dealing with flaws and misdeeds. Otherwise we wouldn't be dwelling on Earth - a planet of trials and atonement. The wrong deeds of past lives still hang over our heads imposing painful experiences upon us. However, this is not a reason for us to go through life fostering a guilt complex.

What distinguishes the woman who induced an abortion is simply a matter of time. She is compromising herself today, as much as we all have compromised ourselves by misbehaving, sometimes in an even worse way, in previous lives.

And if many are forced by the Divine Justice to pay for their crimes through suffering, simply because they did nothing about it, there is always the opportunity of redemption through the practice of Good deeds.

"I desire mercy, not sacrifice" - says Jesus, reminding the Prophet Oseia (Matthew (9:13); we do not have to punish ourselves or wait for the Divine Law to do it in order to redeem our debts. The practice of mercy, through the engagement in good actions, presents itself as a much easier option.

The woman who committed the crime of abortion can perfectly redesign her destiny by working in favor of needy children - adopting a child or helping poor children, being a volunteer in daycare centers, nursery schools and orphanages...

Her efforts towards that will certainly be rewarded by the blessings of Charity and Love, enabling her to renew and readjust her life without traumas and torments.

A DISGUSTING SOLUTION

The word euthanasia, which means "happy death", was created by the philosopher Francis Bacon. His arguments were that the doctor's responsibility is to alleviate illnesses and pain, not only by curing them, but also by granting a peaceful and easy death to the patient when the problem is irreversible.

Although universally considered as homicide, Justice allows euthanasia when applied to dying patients who are suffering terrible pain and afflictions. Law suits filed against people involved in this kind of crime are very unusual.

In some countries, euthanasia is considered an ordinary medical procedure consented by the patient himself or by his family members, with the purpose of shortening the suffering.

Religions in general are against euthanasia, based on two main principles:

First: It is up to God, Lord of our fortune, to promote our return to the Spirit World. In the tablets with the Ten Commandments, given to Moses by God on Mount Sinai, where the fundaments of human justice lie, there is the unquestionable recommendation: "Thou shalt not kill."

Second: Nobody can assure with absolute certainty that a patient is hopelessly unrecoverable. The medical literature is full of examples of patients in desperate conditions who regain their health.

Spiritism confirms such considerations and goes even further by demonstrating that euthanasia not only suspends the purging of the incarnated Spirit provided by the illness, but also imposes serious difficulties on him for his return to the Spiritual World.

André Luiz approaches this subject in the book "Workers of the Eternal Life" written through Francisco Cândido Xavier, by describing Cavalcante's disincarnating process. He was a charitable man who had this unjustified fear of death. Despite his merits and the support of spiritual guides, who assisted him, he simply refused to die, desperately attaching himself to the physical world.

Since the patient was unconscious, and with no family members to consult with, the doctor arbitrarily decided to abbreviate his sufferings with a deadly dose of anesthetics. André Luiz describes:

"Almost immediately the agonizing man silenced. His body started to stiffen slowly, the facial mask became petrified, his moving eyes were soon glassy."

"To a casual observer, Cavalcante could be considered dead - but not to us. The personality of the disincarnating man was linked to the corpse, fully unconscious and unable of any reaction."

Jeronimo, the spiritual mentor who accompanies André Luiz explains:

"Since the massive dose of anesthetic acts directly upon the entire nervous system it also influences the centers of force in the perispirit. Cavalcante is now tied up to trillions of neutralized dormant cells, invaded by a strange sluggishness that makes him unable to react to our assistance. We probably will not be able to release him for the next twelve hours."

In the end, the author emphasizes:

"And just as Jeronimo had predicted, we were only able to release Cavalcante twenty hours later, with a great deal of hardwork. Even so, he was not freed in a favorable and animated condition. He was showing apathy, drowsiness and lack of memory and therefore we conducted him to Fabiano's Nursing Home*, to receive further treatment.

Used since ancient times, euthanasia is far from being a "happy death". It is actually a disgusting solution for the patient, besides being a deplorable disrespect to God's determinations.

---

* Helping institution in the Spiritual World.

OLD TRAUMA

Recommendations:

- Bury me only when I start to stink!

- Do not bury me. I want to be cremated!

- Wait at least twenty-four hours before burying me, no matter the circumstances of my death!

During lectures given about death, a frequent question that arises is:

- If I go through a lethargic trance and wake up in the grave, what will happen to me?

The humorous answer:

- Nothing special. You will die after a few minutes due to lack of oxygen.

* * *

It is amazing how worried people are about the possibility of being buried alive, nurtured by old stories of corpses strangely found turned in the coffin when it is opened months or years after the burial.

Perhaps these facts may have happened in the old centuries, particularly during epidemics or times of battles. There were lots of corpses to be buried and some were not properly checked to see whether the person was really dead. Our ancestors might have taken lethargy for death, thus condemning the victims of their ignorance to die of suffocation.

Today it is practically impossible for this to happen, provided the family requires the presence of a doctor (which in Brazil is compulsory, since you cannot bury someone without a death certificate issued by a doctor; the doctor in turn cannot issue such certificate without examining the corpse.)

A doctor can easily verify whether the person is actually dead or in a lethargic trance. The vital functions do not cease during the lethargic trance, remaining latent and imperceptible to a superficial observation.

He will check with a stethoscope that the blood flow is being kept by the heartbeat. When the heart stops beating death will take place in four minutes. The eye check is also conclusive. If mydriasis occurs, an extreme dilatation of the pupil of the eye with no response to light stimulation, death is consummated.

Seemingly, this type of fear originates from disconnecting problems, since it is very common for the Spirit to remain bonded to the body for a few hours or days after the burial because of a lack of preparation for death.

Considering that all of us, for sure, have already gone through this unpleasant experience in past lives, we keep, hidden in our consciousness, traumas that manifest themselves as a fear of being buried alive.

The understanding of the death mechanism along with the compliance with the present life commitments will help us to overcome this uncomfortable inheritance from disastrous past experiences.

IS IT TIME?

"Only the turkey dies in the eve" the old saying goes, trying to express the fact that nobody disincarnates before his time comes.

In fact, exactly the opposite happens. Only few people use up the time granted to them. With few exceptions, men go through life forcing and unbalancing their physical body.

We destroy the body from outside in with our bad habits, bad temper, and lack of discipline. Alcohol, smoking, drugs, excess of food, as well as lack of exercise, hygiene, adequate rest wear out the body's resistance through the years, shortening physical life.

We destroy the body from inside out by sheltering negative thoughts, grievous ideas, unbalancing feelings such as jealousy, envy, pessimism, hatred, bitterness, loathing... There are people so used to responding with irritation and aggressiveness when they are contradicted, that they eventually "implode" the heart with a sudden heart attack. Others "drown" the immune system in a sea of grief and resentment, depression and anguish, favoring the growth of cancerous tumors.

Such circumstances will fatally give rise to adaptation problems, similar to what happens to an individual who commits suicide. Although the situation of those who disincarnate prematurely due to mental and physical intemperance is less problematic, since they did not intend to die, they are responsible for the damage caused to the physical body and reflected in the perispirit, imposing harsh impressions on it.

As usual, the maladjustment will reverberate in the new physical body when they reincarnate, giving rise to varied disorders and illnesses which are indispensable for readjustment.

We are not the owners of our bodies. We use them temporarily, like someone who rents a car for a long trip. There is a plan to be followed, including itinerary, route, length and maintenance. If we overuse it by lack of discipline and tension, poisoning it with addictions, forgetting the lubricants of optimism and good temper, we will end up facing serious mechanical problems. Besides interrupting the trip and compromising what had been planned, we will be held to account for damaging a vehicle that did not belong to us.

In the future, during a "new trip", we will probably be entitled to a jalopy, with varied limitations, which will require special care and will force us to discipline ourselves.

DANGEROUS GAME

There is a sinister game, of very bad taste, attributed to the Soviets, called "Russian Roulette". The first player is selected, and inserts a bullet in a gun. After that he spins the chambers randomly, puts the barrel against his temples and pulls the trigger. If he hears a click he will breathe relieved and pass the gun on to a partner, who will repeat the ritual. And so they will go on successively until one of them blows his brains out.

A Brazilian variant is the "Paulista Roulette", that has been played by young people in São Paulo for many decades. It consists in crossing a preferential street at high speed, without obeying the stop signs, with powerful bikes. Luck willing the biker may arrive at the other side untouched, otherwise he will be smashed against a car.

Deaths of that sort cannot be considered a fatality. As much as those who push their bodies too hard with their intemperance, these adventure-lovers return prematurely to the Spiritual World, expelled from their own bodies after destroying them with their irresponsibility. They unconsciously commit suicide. They have never really stopped to think that they would end up killing themselves and that they would be held responsible for it.

Something similar happens all over the world with thousands of people who get killed on highways in fatal accidents. Although many of these tragedies can be considered a karma, representing the redemption of old debts, there are many which were not intended to happen, they are the result of imprudence.

In any field of activity there are human and Divine laws to be followed. On highways the former establish speed limits, traffic lanes, signaling, places where turns are allowed, proper places for overtaking. The latter dictate the respect for Life, either our own or the others.

Whenever we fail to comply with them, we become vulnerable to disastrous happenings which impair our existence, mainly when we involve other people.

We are the craftsman of our own destiny and we do it in the short, middle, and long run, day by day through the unfolding of our actions. At an imprudent moment we may hinder our physical existence or even put an end to it before the right time.

Evidently all of that represents experience in a world of trials such as the Earth. The Divine Law harmonizes the events and takes advantage even of our mistakes to teach us something, because we always reap their fruits, learning what to or not to do.

Nevertheless our learning process can be smoother, through good judgment, praying and being aware, as taught in the Gospel. Those who do not do it are playing an "existence roulette", becoming candidates for problems that could be avoided, and sufferings that were not planned.

FUNERALS

When we attend a funeral we fulfill a sacred obligation of sympathy, in an attempt to comfort the family. Unfortunately, we tend to do it by half, only with our physical presence, ignoring what is defined as spiritual behavior, which is expressed through the respect for the place and our efforts to help the dead person.

After a long period of professional mourners, when death was faced as something terrible implying an obligation to suffer, shown through abundant tears, we have ended up at the opposite side, because, except for family members, the bystanders seem to be in a social gathering, where old friends get together to catch up on the latest happenings. People tell jokes and talk about soccer, politics, sex, fashion... Nobody even cares about lowering the tone of voice, an incredible din, which tends to get worse as the burying time approaches, because a greater number of people are present.

The dead person is always remembered with flattering words (at first every dead person is a good one, according to an old human tradition), but eventually the reminiscences head towards the negative aspects of his/her behavior, giving rise to gossip and jokes.

Let us imagine the uncomfortable situation of the Spirit, who, still attached to the body, plunges into an ocean of varied vibrations, the shameful "contribution" of people who attend the funeral in the name of a friendship, but behave as naughty spectators, making the task of a diligent helping group more difficult in their attempt to remove a wounded person from the ruins of a house that has collapsed...

Attached to a temporary residence transformed into physical ruins as a result of death, the disincarnating person, in an unconscious state, receives the impact of such disrespectful and disturbing vibrations that strike him painfully, especially the ones of personal nature. As if in a terrible nightmare, he wants to wake up and regain control of the body, feeling very restless and distressed.

In a funeral attended by many people, with an expressive procession to the grave we can hear:

"What a beautiful funeral! How many people!!"

Nevertheless, not always what seems nice is good, especially when we confront physical and spiritual realities. The greater the number of people the more diverse the talks, the heavier the environment, the greater the impact upon the dead person.

Some time ago I was in a hospital making arrangements for the burial of an indigent person. After everything was settled regarding the necessary documents, the dead person was taken to the cemetery in the hearse with no followers. I myself couldn't make it due to professional commitments.

"How sad! An empty funeral! A lonesome burial!"

Spiritually speaking, it is much better this way. There was nobody to get in the way and the spiritual helpers could accomplish their task in a more peaceful way, freeing the prisoner from a tight jail of flesh and leading him into the glorious spiritual realms.

IDEAL FUNERAL

One time we attended the funeral of a fellow Spiritist. The family, which was also Spiritist, was well aware of the difficulties related to the disconnection and offered him invaluable support and an enlightening example of balance and good behavior that touched many people.

There was no signs of ostentation, only flowers and soothing music which invited to meditation. The widow and children received the condolences with serenity, and discreet tears, relieving the sorrowful trance with perfect understanding of the Divine Wishes. Silence and prayers were requested.

For two or three times, as time elapsed, Spiritist texts related to death were read aloud, emphasizing the situation of the Spirit still attached to the body and warning the people about their responsibilities before someone, on the threshold of Spiritual Life, a bird about to leave the cage, which has fragile wings and understandable restraints, problems that might be minimized or worsened by the bystanders.

Before the coffin was closed, at the scheduled time, someone spoke briefly about the meaning of death, improperly considered the end of life, when it is only another side of it, at grander horizons, inaccessible to the human sight, emphasizing a curious contradiction:

In the physical dimension, the feeling of personal loss, the sad atmosphere, the painful absence...

In the spiritual dimension the happiness of family and friends in the anticipation of a happy reunion...

Next, the lecturer invited everybody to pray, addressing his word to Jesus, the divine intermediary of everybody's affection and solicitude towards the passenger to Eternity, wishing him lots of peace and a happy return to the Spiritual World.

Those who know the problems related to disincarnation have the obligation to contribute so that the funerals become a place of a great deal of respect and good behavior.

We can start with our own behavior. Let us be respectful. Let us cultivate silence, speaking, if necessary, in a low tone of voice, in an uplifting way. Let us talk about the dead person with discretion, avoiding to overload him with recollections and feelings capable of disturbing him, mainly if death took place under tragic circumstances. And let us pray a lot in his benefit.

If we are not able to behave in such a way, it is better to go away, avoiding an increase in the disrespectful choir of voices and vibrations that disturb the dead person so acutely.

FOR HIS SAKE*

Dear Friend,

If you cultivate a religious principle, you know death is not the end. The eternal spirit, with its potentialities of love and the feeling that shapes its individuality, simply leaves the jail of flesh, like a butterfly that leaves the cocoon, heading into the horizon.

---

* We give out this message at funerals in Bauru with good receptivity. Due to heterogeneity of belief, we avoid a very clear approach about the difficulties of disconnection.

Few, however, are ready for the grand journey. Not many exercise the wings of virtue and unselfishness.

Therefore, it is natural for the dead person to face difficulties in trying to adapt to the new spiritual reality, mainly when they cannot count on the support of those who attend the funeral during the long hours that precede the burying.

The murmuring of silly talks and less uplifting comments, as well as the instability due to nonacceptance and despair, reflect in his consciousness, imposing painful impressions.

If someone is very dear to your heart, consider the fact that he needs your courage and your trust in God. If you do not accept the separation, questioning God's Wishes, your despair affects him, unmercifully, like a devastating storm of anguish.

If it is the friend that you admire so much, for whom you nourish special feelings, pay him a silent homage, respecting the solemn transition which is defining new paths for him...

If your presence is inspired on an obligation of sympathy, offer him, in the quietness of your heart, a charitable prayer, simple and spontaneous, to cheer him up.

Remember that one day you will also be in the same situation, lying in a coffin and, still attached to earthly impressions, you will eager for people to respect your memory and not to disrupt your disconnection, supporting you with valuable silence and prayers, serenity and understanding, so that you can safely cross the threshold of Eternal Life.

THE GARMENT IN THE CLOSET

The most thrilling scenes from a horror movie, those that give us the "goose bumps" usually show coffins and corpses.

This is the result of filmmakers who exploit the morbid and atavistic fear of death, to satisfy those that nurture a strange pleasure in being scared. But as they start to understand that the coffin is merely a wooden box lined with cloth and that the corpse is nothing more than a flesh garment of someone who, after an earthly period, went back to its home world - The Spiritual World, they will go about choosing other themes.

It would be ridiculous to feel goose bumps when you saw the contents of a closet or, inside it the garment of an absent family member. Nevertheless, that is exactly what happens to many people in relation to death. We know people who systematically refuse to attend funerals, being averse to coffins and corpses, even of family members, dominated by an indescribable fear. They probably carry traumas related to tragic occurrences in previous lives.

For a vast majority, however, the problem stems from an inadequate way of facing the great transition, especially due to the information received during the childhood years.

I remember that in my young years, many times I was asked to kiss dead family members, which I did with lots of embarrassment, not relishing the contact of my lips with that cold, pale and rigid face of someone whom I had known full of life, with whom I had lived, and who now was inert, solemn, somber... And I let myself be influenced by the desperate tears and painful moaning of those less controlled, building in my head the idea that death is something terrible and frightening, a disgusting image that only in my adult life I was able to get rid of through the Spiritist knowledge.

Extreme care must be dedicated to children, making them familiar with the idea that we are eternal spiritual beings, wearing a fleshly garment that one day we will have to abandon, just like we abandon a worn out garment after some time of use.

That is the way the corpse has to be shown to children, when they want to see it, explaining, through simple images, suitable for their understanding that grandpa, auntie, daddy or any other disincarnated family member is now living in another place, where he/she will have a new and much better garment.

Equally important is the example of serenity and self-control from the adults, offering to the little ones a more suitable image of death, showing it as a temporary separation from someone who has not died, but only left.

WARNINGS FROM BEYOND

Dr. Flávio Pinheiro, a dedicated Spiritist doctor from Ibitinga (a city in the State of São Paulo) came to me.

- Richard, I am here to invite you for a "funeral duty".

- ?!

- I want you to "bless my soul" through a prayer before the burying. And ask everybody not to disturb me with their moaning and sadness.

- Come off it, Doctor! You are not going to die so soon! You still have many debts to pay off!...

- Yes, my dear friend, I am a big sinner. Nevertheless, I am going to disincarnate anyway. I must undergo a delicate and immediate cardiac surgery in the city of São Paulo and I am sure that I am on my way to the Spiritual World.

In spite of condemning his pessimism, I agreed to fulfill his insistent request.

A few days later I was asked to do as I had promised. Dr. Flávio Pinheiro had died during the surgery.

* * *

The wedding was going to be simple, no reception. Only family members and a few friends. Among them, the young bride insisted on the presence of a very dear one: Caetano Aielo, an elderly Spiritist from the city of Bauru.

- When is it going to be? - asked the guest.

- In three months.

- Oh! Then I cannot make it!...

- You are going to insult me?! I will get mad at you! Your presence is indispensable! Cancel any other commitments!

- This commitment I cannot cancel, my dear. The "people up there" are giving me intuition that I will leave soon...

Two months later Caetano Aielo, who did not have any health problems, got sick, and in no time, died.

* * *

These are examples of premonition. The person feels a strong impression when something is about to happen (first case) or feels warned about it (second case).

Just like many animals have mechanisms that allow them to feel a storm or an earthquake approaching, before any manifestation of it, there are people especially sensitive to future occurrences. This is instinctive in them.

As regards death, premonition is frequently influenced by Spiritual Benefactors, aiming at helping the person who will disincarnate and his family members. Though scary, it psychologically prepares those involved in the event, so they will not be taken by surprise, or feel shocked about it.

The premonition is especially comforting in the event of tragic disincarnation such as in traffic accidents. It makes it possible for the family to understand that nothing happened by chance, or even worse, unnecessarily. It was simply the fulfillment of Divine Wishes, in the course of human trials.

STRANGE CULT

- Hello, going for a walk?

- Yeah, I'm going to visit my son...

- What?! Has he not died?!

- I'm going to the cemetery...

* * *

This surrealist dialog frequently takes place. People visit dead persons in the cemetery. They take flowers and affectionately take care of the grave, the "last dwelling".

Certain religious cults even advise their followers to take food to the cemetery. And there is the traditional burning of candles, to "light the paths of beyond".

At a certain time in my childhood, some friends and I, naughty boys, went to the cemetery to "steal" candles to play with.

When my grandmother, a very dear old Italian woman, learned about it, she, who was very zealous about religious traditions, collected them all and after scolding me severely for the lack or respect, lit them in her porch.

- Candles for the intention of Souls - she explained solemnly - have to be burned to the end!

I thanked the Heavens above for her having given up the idea of making me go back to the cemetery during the night to give the lit candles back to their owners. With her typical generosity, she accepted the argument that it would be impossible to identify the exact graves from which they were taken.

There are incredible misconceptions about this subject. Many people cannot fully grasp the idea that the eternal Spirit follows its destiny in the Spiritual World, leaving in the cemetery only the fleshly garment in decomposition, which means nothing to its individuality, the same way that a suit worn by a person is not the person himself.

Visits to the cemetery are, therefore, an authentic cult of the corpse, which tends to disappear as the human creatures start to assimilate broader concepts about the spiritual life.

It is necessary to emphasize that when we think too much about those who have left us we are calling out to them, bringing them close to us.

Thus, let us not transform the cemeteries in "living rooms for the dead". There are nicer places for this contact, especially for the dead person. If he disincarnated recently and is not well suited to the new realities, he will not feel at ease in contemplating the remains of his flesh.

FLOWERS FOR THE DEAD

If we intend to cultivate the memory of dear family members, transferred to the Spiritual World, let us choose the ideal place: our home.

Let us use many flowers to decorate Life, in the comfort of our homes; never to praise Death, in the coldness of a cemetery.

They will invariably prefer to receive our message of affection through the post office of longing, with no mournful stamp.

It is good to miss someone. It means that there is love in our hearts, the supreme feeling that lends meaning and purpose to our existence.

When we truly love someone, with a pure and unselfish feeling, exemplified best in the love of Mothers, we feel strong and resolute, willing to face the World.

Maybe God has invented the illusion of death for us to overcome the age-old tendency of restricting love to selfish closed family circles, teaching us how to nurture it as a whole, struggling for fraternity working for the benefit of our mates which leads us into nobler achievements.

Let us not permit, therefore, that the longing for somebody be transformed into a reason for anguish and oppression. Let us use the filters of trust and faith, making it tender through the understanding that the loving bonds do not end at the grave. LOVE, the essence of Life, spreads, without limits, to the Infinite dwellings, a subtle bridge that sustains, enduringly, the communion between Heaven and Earth.

Thus, there are two reasons for us not to nurture sadness:

We miss somebody - we are not dead...

Our beloved ones are not dead - they miss us...

And if we are able to pray, contrite and serene, these moments of evocation will moisten the flowers of absence with the blessing of hope, we will then be able to feel their presence among us, tenderly enveloping our hearts with the perfumes of joy and peace.

CREMATION

The fear of being buried alive makes many people talk about being cremated. The corpse is incinerated, thus avoiding the problem. But there is one doubt which is a very frequent question in our lectures about death:

- What will happen if during the cremation I am still attached to the body?

In these circumstances I usually say:

- Well, inside the oven the temperature reaches one thousand and four hundred degrees Celsius. If you take into consideration the fact that the water boils at a hundred degrees, we can imagine what that is. It gets so hot that the corpse itself starts a combustion process. Then, among the flames, if the dead person is influenced by medieval theological beliefs he will imagine: My God! I'm in Hell!"

Of course, this is just a joke to cheer up the listeners in face of such a mournful subject. Any enlightened person, from any religion knows that the Hell of Fire where the souls burn in eternal torments without being destroyed is a fantasy created in remote times when religious beliefs were imposed more through fear than through logic. Today we know that Heaven and Hell are not geographical places. They exist inside each one of us as a result of our actions.

Objectively speaking we could answer the question by saying that if the Spirit is attached to the body we will not go through pains, because the corpse cannot transmit any sensation to the Spirit, but obviously he will experience very unpleasant impressions, besides the trauma of a violent and impromptu disconnection. It is a good opportunity to highlight some considerations by Emmanuel, in the book "The Consoler", written through Francisco Cândido Xavier.

"During cremation it is mandatory to be merciful with the corpse, postponing the act of destruction of the flesh for a longer time, since, in a certain way, there are always many echoes of sensitivity between the disincarnated Spirit and the Body, in which the vital tone has been extinguished. During the first hours that follow the disconnection the organic fluids still imprison the soul in the feelings of the material existence."

Francisco Cândido, in an interview for television in 1971, transmits new information coming from Emmanuel*. At least seventy-two hours should elapse before cremation. As it seems, this time is enough for the disconnection to take place, except in cases of deaths involving suicide or people too bonded to addictions and human interests.

In the crematory ovens in São Paulo, there is a legal waiting period of 24 hours. Nevertheless, the regulations allow the corpse to be kept in the refrigerated chamber as long as the family wishes. Spiritists usually ask for three days. Some people ask for seven days.

---

* This is part of the book *"CHICO XAVIER - FROM HIPPIES TO THE PROBLEMS OF THE WORLD"*, chapter 18.

It is important to realize, however, that more important than all these precautions is to live a balanced life, marked by the effort for self-renewal and the practice of good deeds, so that, under any circumstance of our death, we will be freed promptly, with no traumas and no worries about the destiny of our body.

TRANSPLANTS

The advances of Medicine regarding surgical techniques and the discovery of new drugs that eliminate or reduce rejection open up grand horizons for the transplant of organs. In big surgical centers, transplants of cornea, bones, skin, cartilage, and vessels are routine. Transplants of heart, kidney and liver, considered impossible some decades ago, are increasing. This way, just like blood banks, there are now cornea, bone, and skin banks...

Considering the fact that the Spirit is not disconnected immediately after death, some doubts arise: Will the Spirit feel the pain? Will he have marks of it in the perispirit? Will the person who donates his eyes suffer from sight problems in the Spiritual World?

Usually the surgical procedure does not impose pain on the deceased person. As we have already said, agony is like a kind of general anesthetics to the dying person, reflecting in the Spirit, which tends to sleep in the crucial moments of the grand transition. Even if conscious, the collapsing body usually does not transmit feelings of pain.

There aren't traumatizing reflexes in the spiritual body as a result of physical body mutilation. The person who donates his eyes will not enter the Spiritual World as a blind one. If it were so, what would happen to those whose body is destroyed by fire or disintegrates during an explosion?

The integrity of the perispirit is intimately connected to the life we lead and not to the kind of death we have or the destination given to our bodily remains.

In this regard, it is always important to emphasize that the greatest violence that affects our perispirit, making us plunge into the hell of agony and pain, is suicide.

Nevertheless, regarding transplants there is still one problem to be solved: when vital organs such as the heart and the liver are involved, the surgery has to take place as soon as the cerebral death occurs (when the brain ceases working), before clinical death, when the heart stops beating.

As we see it, this procedure is similar to a euthanasia, since clinical death does not always happen right after the cerebral death.

For these transplants, the organs of people who have had accidents, including vascular ones, are used. It is not possible to use the organs of people who die because of old age or after being sick for long periods. To the benefit of the person who has had an accident, it is important after the cerebral death to let Nature follow its course and to allow the clinical death to come spontaneously. A few hours, days or weeks in this situation, despite the pressure on and anguish of the family, will favor a less traumatic disincarnation of the Spirit.

In the future, Medicine will surely develop techniques which will allow the removal of such organs for donation **after the occurrence** of death, without drastic measures that might complicate the disincarnating process.

BLESSED CHARITY

One of the most simple transplants, with minimum problems of rejection and with extremely positive results is the one of the cornea.

The surgery for the removal of the donor's cornea is fast, leaving no external marks, and may be accomplished up to six hours after death, which avoids the problem mentioned in the previous chapter.

Everybody can donate his corneas, with no limitations as to age, or circumstances of death. Provided the corneas are not damaged by any kind of lesion, they might be used.

To become a donor, you can refer to a cornea bank (they usually are located at hospitals).

At the same time, it is important to tell family members about the procedures in the event of our death. Above all, it is important to make them understand that they cannot oppose our wishes about the body we are leaving behind. Our will has to be respected.

This measure is extremely important, because somebody will have to consent to the surgery and it is very common for no one to be willing to do it. Age-old superstitions about death prevail at that moment. Many consider the act of using organs from a dead person a profanation, being entangled in old conditionings.

Besides being an act of courage, getting rid of rooted prejudice, the donation of a cornea is a blessed act of charity. Let us imagine our happiness in the Spiritual World when we learn that our modest gift - a small piece of a worn-out garment, has provided someone with the most precious of all treasures - the ability to see!

And undoubtedly there will be closer attention paid by the Spiritual Benefactors, in the sense of avoiding that our generosity causes us some kind of embarrassment, providing us, also, ways to overcome the problems of adapting to the new realities of Spirit Life more easily.

To illustrate this we can use the example of the young Wladimir Cezar Ranieri, described in the book "Amor e Saudade" (Love and Longing), organized by Rubens Silvio Germinhasi, with messages written through Francisco Cândido Xavier.

Wladimir donated his eyes, which were extracted after his death caused by himself with a shot in the chest. We will transcribe some parts of the message that the young man wrote to his parents, where he mentions the benefits he received as a donor, despite his insane act:

"I know that I have entered a nightmare where I saw my own blood running down my chest as if that red stream was never going to end."

"The person who commits suicide is imprisoned but not behind bars."

"I admit that some fellows with similar problems see themselves imprisoned with no cuffs or bars, because nobody can escape from one's own consciousness."

"Thank God, I recovered from the endless hemorrhage which was driving me crazy. After some weeks of suffering, a doctor came to me with good news."

"He told me that the prayers from a person that had benefited from the cornea I had donated to the cornea bank had been converted into a small compress which, placed on my chest exactly where the bullet had entered, made the flow of blood cease immediately. And although I had never been good to others and had always omitted myself when it was time to be useful, I could finally understand that the good deeds, even when done involuntarily by a dead person, are able to restore the strengths of our existence."

CURIOUS OBSESSION

The afflictions and sorrows that arise from the death of a beloved one, when the powerful resources of prayer and acceptance are not used, may generate many health problems. If we refuse to lead a normal life, taking up the day-by-day routines and cultivating a pleasure for life, we will certainly suffer from physical and psychological disorders.

However strange it might sound, the presence of the dead person may contribute to this. Being unprepared for the new realities of Spirit Life and ignoring his present state, he goes back to his home and tends to associate with the family members through mediumship. That is why many people feel the same symptoms of the disease that afflicted the dead person. If the person died due to severe lung crisis, they feel pain in their chest, oppression, and feel shortness of breath...

This happens because the connection established with the dead person transmits impressions, not yet overcome, related to the end of his existence. The dead person acts like a sleepwalker who speaks and hears, feeling disturbed because nobody pays attention to him.

Medical treatment might help, but does not solve the problem, because it deals only with the effects without examining the causes. The Spiritist Doctrine, which is in the forefront of this subject, offers many resources for the treatment of both parts:

The living person benefits in a Spiritist Center by receiving a magnetic transfer - passes of the hands, fluidic water, orientation on how to face death, and an objective view about the human existence.

The disincarnated person, who is magnetically attached to the sick person, also comes to the meeting and receives valuable assistance from the Spiritual Benefactors, especially through the communication made possible by the presence of mediums. The contact with the physical energies of the medium gives new strengths to the dead person and he experiences moments of lucidity, like someone who has awakened from a long sleep, becoming capable of understanding.

This is the end of the obsessive process, involuntarily caused by the disincarnated person in an attempt to seek help, support, attention...

It should be noted that, more often than not, the disincarnated person is more obsessed than he is obsessor. Helpless and unprepared for the Spirit Life, he is attracted by the family members when they refuse to overcome the anguish from separation, starting a mental fixation process which confuses and holds back the disincarnated person, even when he is willing to follow his way in the Spiritual World.

Therefore, it is as important to enlighten the Spirits who disturb the family as it is to teach the family so as not to disturb the Spirits.

THE MOST IMPORTANT

Should we tell a terminal patient about his situation? Doesn't he have the right to know that he is sentenced to death, that he is about to die? Wouldn't this help him prepare for the great transition? These questions are hard to answer since very few people are willing to face reality with serenity.

Fear, insecurity, attachment to physical life and family are some of the common reactions of people before death, causing serious obstacles for the spiritual disconnection, like the dweller of a house in ruins who refuses to admit the need to leave it behind.

In the most critical situations, it is common for the patient to create illusions about himself, nurturing the hope that he will get better. This occurs even to very intelligent and literate people, with total capacity of understanding that they are near the end.

As part of a group who renders spiritual assistance, I visited for some time a terminally sick person. He was an elderly gentleman with serious circulatory problems. In spite of being weak and imprisoned in a bed since his last stroke, he showed lucidity, and with satisfaction he received us to study "The Gospel According to Spiritism", to pray, to receive magnetic healing and to drink the fluidic water.

When commenting about the text we had just read, we tried to talk about death, defining it as a letter granting freedom to the Spirit. And subtly we emphasized that the elderly are nearer the great transition and should prepare themselves for the return to the Spiritual World, cultivating detachment and trust in God. Even without being able to speak, the sick man moved his hands vigorously trying to mimic the idea that he did not intend to die.

On other occasions, while taking care of family members in similar situation, I felt the same resistance. At crucial moments, very near the end, they claimed that their problem was not so bad and with the help of God they would get over it.

We inevitably conclude that if the sick person does not want to admit his precarious condition, if he resists the prospect of death, if he tries to fool himself with the idea of his recovery, it is better not to counter him.

The most important thing is to offer care and attention. Both extremes of life are the same. Just like the newborn, the disincarnating person is extremely dependent, both at physical and emotional levels. He needs special care, and above all, he desperately needs to feel loved, to know that people worry about him, that he is not considered a burden.

There is nothing sadder than a lonesome terminal patient, put into a hospital bed, where the people whom he loved most go as visitors. They feel very touched by the person's suffering, but they are always in a hurry because of other commitments.

They cannot understand that the most important commitment is to be near that Spirit about to leave the Earth, offering him the blessings of their presence, their thoughtfulness, and consideration!

ROOTS OF STABILITY

According to research carried out by the magazine "Psychology Today" the thing people fear the most is the death of a beloved person. Many people simply refuse to think about it, even in relation to older family members. As regards kids, forget about it!...

There is a human tendency of setting the roots of emotional stability on the grounds of endearment, especially towards family members.

We feel safer this way, willing to face the hardships of existence.

The problem, though, is that at the death of someone very close to a person's heart, he loses balance, as if the ground had been removed from under his feet, and lives a crisis of despair. For a long time he feels emotionally mutilated, with no support, no courage, no will to live...

To avoid such problem, we have to learn how to cope with death, accepting it as an evolutionary experience typical of the world in which we live and that, most probably, before it comes after us, it might take someone we love within a few years or within a few days.

We should always be prepared, that is, think about the possibility without morbidity or pessimism, but exercising our capacity of being realistic.

We are not saying that we should be rationally cold, reducing our affections to mere pieces of a game we agree to lose during the game of destiny, but we should seek understanding of Life's mechanisms, so that we do not feel useless, as if there were no more reasons to live because we have lost a beloved person.

Arrival and departure, company and loneliness, union and separation, life and death, these are all existential antitheses that keep on being repeated throughout the centuries, shaping our personality in the dynamics of evolution, according to the wise and just Divine Will.

Therefore, to our own benefit, it is mandatory that we set other emotional roots, starting with our effort to comply with the purposes of our earthly journey. Living with beloved ones is important, but it represents only one of the motivations that we must have in life. There are others, immediate and essential: our moral and intellectual improvement, the effort for self-renewal, active social participation through good deeds, nurturing spiritual values... Similar initiatives light in our hearts the divine flame of ideals that light the ways, offering us comfort and safety in all situations.

When we have an ideal, assuming our responsibility as sons of God, created to His image, developing our creative potentials, we become more capable of loving, we have better relationships with family members, we tighten the bonds of affinity, but detachment will mark our affective feelings, making us capable of keeping balance and tranquillity when death comes after someone of our intimate circle.

RETURNED JEWELS

There is a key word that helps us face the death of a loved one with serenity and balance: submission.

It expresses our willingness to accept what is inevitable, considering that the sovereign will of God prevails above human will, who offers us the experience of death in favor of the improvement of our lives.

About this topic, it is appropriate to remember an ancient oriental story about a rabbi, Jewish religious preacher, who led a very happy life with his virtuous wife and two admirable sons, intelligent and diligent boys, loving and disciplined.

Due to his activities he once had to be absent from home for many days, embarking on a long journey. In the meantime, a serious accident caused the death of the two boys.

We can imagine the suffering of that mother!.. Nevertheless, she was a strong woman. Comforted by her faith and unshakable trust in God, she bravely bore the strain. Her greatest worry was about the husband. How would she tell him what had happened?!... She was afraid that a strong commotion would have fatal consequences, because he had a cardiac insufficiency. She prayed a lot, pleading for inspiration from Heaven. The Lord did not leave her without an answer...

A few days later, the rabbi returned home. He arrived in the afternoon after a long trip, but he was happy. He tenderly embraced his wife and soon asked about the boys...

- Do not worry, my dear. They will come later. Bathe yourself, while I prepare something for you to eat.

A while later, at the table, they were talking about everyday events, in those typical moments of a loving couple after a brief separation.

- How about the boys? They are taking too long!...

- Forget about them... I need your help to solve a serious problem...

- What's the matter? I have noticed that you are depressed!... Tell me! We will find a solution together, inspired by God!...

- When you traveled, a friend of ours came to me and asked me to take care of two pieces of jewelry of incalculable value. They are extremely precious! I had never seen anything like that! And the problem is that he is coming to pick them up and I am not willing to give them back.

- What has gotten into you, darling! You are not being yourself! You have never nurtured frailties!...

- That's because I had never seen such jewelry. They are divine, wonderful!...

- But they do not belong to you...

- I cannot bear the thought of losing them!...

- Nobody loses something one does not have. To keep them would be the same as stealing!

- Help me!...

- Of course I will. We will go together to give them back today!

- Well, my dear, thy will be done. The treasure will be returned. In fact, it already has. The pieces of jewelry were our sons. God, who trusted them to us as a loan, has come to fetch them!...

The rabbi understood the message and, although experiencing the anguish that such separation imposed upon him, he overcame any strong reaction, capable of causing him harm.

Husband and wife embraced each other very touched, mixing the tears that slowly rolled down their faces, without words of revolt or despair, and in one voice they repeated Job's sacred words:

"The Lord gave, and The Lord hath taken away: blessed be the name of the Lord."

PASSPORT

"Learn how to live well, and you shall know how to die well"

(Confucius)

After presenting the lecture about death in a city in the state of Rio Grande do Sul, Brazil, when I was answering the audience's questions, a girl commented:

"The subject impresses me a whole lot. That is why I decided to attend this lecture, even though I am not a Spiritist. I must confess, however, that after your enlightenment, I, who had always been afraid of death, am now terrified!..."

Fortunately, this picturesque confession is an exception. Since the fear of death is usually a consequence of lack of information, I have noticed that many people are able to face it with serenity when they learn about the subject.

Nevertheless, it is essential to recognize that we will only overcome the fear of death for good when we adjust our lives to the spiritual realities unveiled by the Spiritist Doctrine, trying to define the meaning of the human existence.

As Eternal Spirits, temporarily imprisoned within the flesh, we cannot forget that our ultimate and legitimate dwelling is located in the Spiritual Realms, where we will continue our trials as we overcome the need for incarnation in dense worlds such as the Earth, where the difficulties and limitations act like sand paper necessary for trimming off our grosser flaws.

If we turn our incarnation into a vacation resort, marked by laziness and indifference; if we face it as a casino for irresponsible gambling of emotions; if we aim at an artificial heaven sustained by vices and passions; if we experience well-being and safety on the mischievous grounds of immediate interests, ignoring the purposes of existence, we will fatally be afraid of death. After all, we will leave all that behind. And something tells us, deep down inside, that we will be held responsible for compromising our life and for our lack of preparation for death.

Those who wander around unaware of the purposes of the reincarnation journey, will find out, hopelessly and sadly, that death, a freeing angel that should unveil wonderful spiritual horizons, has only uncovered the heavy burdens that they have placed upon themselves, by making their existence a constant act of inconsequence, postponing the effort for self renewal.

To our benefit, it is essential that we become aware of eternity, knowing that we are not mere groups of cells with intelligence, biological beings that had their origin in the cradle and will disappear in the grave.

We are Eternal Spirits! We already existed before the cradle and will continue to exist after the grave! We must live in accordance with this truth, leaving behind petty illusions so that we can be free and determined in search of inalienable values of virtue and knowledge, our passport for the glorious dwellings in the Infinite!

It is hard to determine when we are going to be summoned to the Spiritual Realms. Death is like a thief. Nobody knows how, when, and where it will come. The ideal is to be always ready, living each day as if it were the last one, taking full advantage of the time we have in a disciplined and productive effort to offer the best of ourselves in favor of human improvement. That way we can be sure to have a happy return to our Spiritual Nation, as the old oriental proverb goes:

"When you were born, you cried and the world rejoiced. Live your life so that when you die, the world cries and you rejoice."

OTHER TITLES FROM THE AUTHOR

PARA VIVER A GRANDE MENSAGEM
(To live the great message)

TEMAS DE HOJE, PROBLEMAS DE SEMPRE
(Themes from today, problems from forever)

A VOZ DO MONTE
(The voice from the Mount)

ATRAVESSANDO A RUA
(Crossing the street)

EM BUSCA DO HOMEM NOVO
(In search of a new man)
*In association with Sérgio Lourenço
and Therezinha Oliveira.*

ENDEREÇO CERTO
(The right address)

A CONSTITUIÇÃO DIVINA
(The Divine Constitution)

UMA RAZÃO PARA VIVER
(A reason to live)

UM JEITO DE SER FELIZ
(A way of being happy)

ENCONTROS E DESENCONTROS
(Adventures and misadventures)

QUEM TEM MEDO DOS ESPÍRITOS?
(Who is afraid of Spirits?)

A FORÇA DAS IDÉIAS
(The power of ideas)

QUEM TEM MEDO DA OBSESSÃO
(Who is afraid of obsession?)

VIVER EM PLENITUDE
(Living in plenitude)

VENCENDO A MORTE E A OBSESSÃO
(Overcoming death and obsession)

TEMPO DE DESPERTAR
(Time to awaken)

NÃO PISE NA BOLA
(Don't go astray)

A PRESENÇA DE DEUS
(The presence of God)

FUGINDO DA PRISÃO
(Running away from prison)

O VASO DE PORCELANA
(The porcelain vase)

O CÉU AO NOSSO ALCANCE
(Heaven within reach)

PAZ NA TERRA
(Peace on Earth)

ESPIRITISMO, UMA NOVA ERA
(Spiritism, a new Era)

O DESTINO EM SUAS MÃOS
(Destiny in your hands)